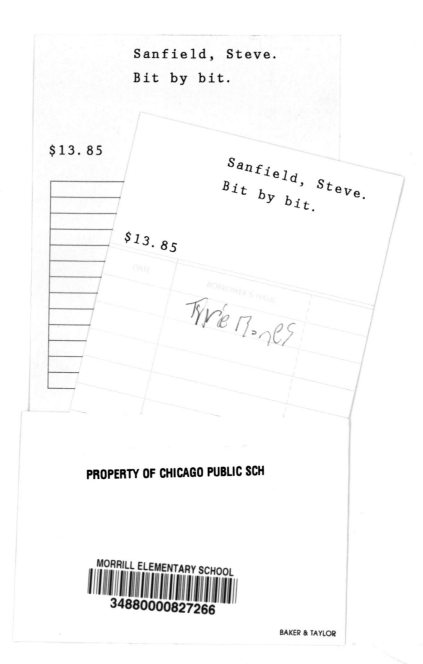

Sanfield, Steve.
Bit by bit.

$13.85

Sanfield, Steve.
Bit by bit.

$13.85

DATE	BORROWER'S NAME	
	Tyre Mones	

PROPERTY OF CHICAGO PUBLIC SCH

BIT by BIT

STEVE SANFIELD

ILLUSTRATED BY
SUSAN GABER

PAPERSTAR

Penguin Putnam Books for Young Readers

Text copyright © 1995 by Steve Sanfield. Illustrations copyright © 1995 by Susan Gaber. All rights reserved.

This book, or parts thereof, may not be reproduced in any form without permission in writing from the publisher. A PaperStar Book, published in 1999 by Penguin Putnam Books for Young Readers, 345 Hudson Street, New York, NY 10014. PaperStar is a registered trademark of The Putnam Berkley Group, Inc. The PaperStar logo is a trademark of The Putnam Berkley Group, Inc.

Originally published in 1995 by Philomel Books. Published simultaneously in Canada. Printed in the United States of America.

Book Design by Gunta Alexander. The text is set in Weiss.

Library of Congress Cataloging-in-Publication Data

Sanfield, Steve. Bit by bit / Steve Sanfield; illustrated by Susan Gaber. p. cm. Summary: When Zundel the tailor wears out his beautiful coat, he continues to make smaller and smaller garments from the material that is left. [1. Clothing and dress—Fiction.] I. Gaber, Susan, ill. II. Title. PZ7.S2237Bi 1995 [E]—dc20 94-8752 CIP AC ISBN 0-698-11775-1

10 9 8 7 6 5 4 3 2 1

To Aaron.—S.S.

For Vicki and Marty.—S.G.

I am a storyteller,
which means that
I tell stories—
all kinds of stories—
serious stories and funny stories,
cloudy stories and sunny stories.

Right now,
I'm going to
tell you a story
about an old friend of mine
who I've never met but
who I know quite well.

His name is Zundel
and he lives
across many seas
in a small village
neither you nor I
have ever been to.

Zundel is a tailor, a poor tailor.
He earns his daily bread
by sewing and stitching,
mending and fixing
coats and caps
and dresses and wraps
for the likes of you and me.

Zundel once had
a long winter coat.
He wore it in the morning
and he wore it at night.
He wore it so much
that
bit by bit
he wore it out.

Zundel continued to
sew and stitch
and mend and fix
until
bit by bit
he saved enough pennies
to buy himself
a beautiful piece of cloth.

The cloth had
red threads and gold threads,
blue threads and green threads,
and from that cloth
Zundel the Tailor
made himself
another
long winter coat.

How Zundel loved that coat.
He wore it in the morning
and he wore it at night.
He wore it and wore it
and wore it and wore it
until
bit by bit
he
w—o—r—e
it
out.

Of course
he was sad,
but when he looked
he saw
there was enough
of that beautiful cloth
with the red threads and the gold threads,
the blue threads and the green threads
to make himself
a
jacket.

How Zundel loved that jacket.
He wore it in the morning
and he wore it at night.
He wore it and wore it
and wore it and wore it
until
bit by bit
he
w—o—r—e
it
out.

Zundel
was even sadder this time,
but when he looked
he saw there was enough
of that beautiful cloth
with the red threads and the gold threads,
the blue threads and the green threads
to make himself
a
vest.

How Zundel loved that vest.
He wore it in the morning
and he wore it at night.
He wore it and wore it
and wore it and wore it
until
bit by bit
he
w——o——r——e
it
out.

Our poor tailor
almost cried.
He was sure
there couldn't be anything left,
but when he looked
he saw
there was still enough
of that beautiful cloth
with the red threads and the gold threads,
the blue threads and the green threads
to make himself
a
cap.

How Zundel loved that cap.
He wore it in the morning
and he wore it at night.
He wore it and wore it
and wore it and wore it
until
bit by bit
he
w———o———r———e
it
out.

Zundel
did cry this time.
He was absolutely sure
there couldn't be anything left,
but when he looked
he saw
there was still enough
of that beautiful cloth
with the red threads and the gold threads,
the blue threads and the green threads
to make himself
a
pocket.

How Zundel loved that pocket.
He wore it in the morning
and he wore it at night.
He wore it and wore it
and wore it and wore it
until
bit by bit
he
w———o———r———e
it
out.

Through his tears
Zundel the Tailor held his breath.
Surely there could be nothing left,
but when he looked
he saw
there was just barely enough
of that beautiful cloth
with the red threads and the gold threads,
the blue threads and the green threads
to make himself
a
button.

How Zundel loved that button.
He loved it more than his coat.
He loved it more than his jacket.
He loved it more than his vest.
He loved it more than his cap.
He loved it more than his pocket.
He loved it so much that
he wore it in the morning
and he wore it at night.
He wore it and wore it
and wore it and wore it
until
bit by bit
he
w———————o————————r————————e
it
out.

Zundel
was absolutely
completely
one hundred percent certain
there could be nothing left,
and when he looked
he saw
he was right.
There was nothing left.
But…

when I looked,
I saw
there was still just enough
of that beautiful cloth
with the red threads and the gold threads,
the blue threads and the green threads
for me
to begin
this story
all over again.

A NOTE ABOUT THIS STORY

"If I Had a Little Coat" is one of the songs my grandmother of the long red hair used to hum and sing to me when I was a child. It was among the dozens of Yiddish and Russian folk songs she carried with her from her village deep in the Pale of Settlement when she came to America almost a century ago. Now the song has transformed itself and found new life here as a story. Listen to it. Tell it yourself.   —S.S.